City Guide to Baku

Stephen Stocks

CONTENTS

Foreword

The largest and most dynamic city in the Caucasus, Baku is often overlooked by visitors in favour of its neighbours Tbilisi and Yerevan. Yet it is far and away the most exciting destination in the region, and deserves to be high up on any history-lover's bucket list. The city is booming, and while some liken it to its brash Middle Eastern cousin, Dubai, it offers much more than just glittering skyscrapers and marble-clad shopping centres. Baku has witnessed almost two millennia of tumultuous history and has been witness to the rise and fall of a succession of empires, and this has left its mark on the city you see today.

Baku's beautifully-preserved old town harbours ancient mosques, palaces, towers, caravanserais and hammams within the confines of imposing twelfth-century defensive walls. The city has been home over time to Zoroastrians, Arabs, Ottomans, Persians, Shirvants and Russians, and each has left their indelible mark. Spreading out from the shores of the Caspian Sea, leafy boulevards lined with oil boom-era mansions give the feel of a European capital, with glitzy boutiques and Mercedes aplenty. Elsewhere, grey Soviet-era apartment blocks jostle for space with a Zaha Hadid-designed architectural masterpiece. Rusting railway tracks and nodding donkey oil wells encircle a centuries-old

Zoroastrian fire temple. Hillsides burn and mud volcanoes bubbles. Baku is all this and much more; a vibrant mix of heady flavours, from different cultures, religion and periods. Only by diving deep into its treasures can you truly appreciate it.

The good news is that now is the perfect time to visit. Baku offers a modern, traveller-friendly infrastructure, with a wide selection of hotels and restaurants catering to every taste. Public transport stretches into every corner of the city, making it easy and cost-effective to see all the sights. And what's even better, the visa regime has been significantly relaxed, with many nationalities eligible to apply for e-visas. So now's the time to visit, and this book will be your companion as you explore the city. Welcome to Baku.

About this guide

This easy-to-use city guide helps you to unearth Baku's treasures. Organised around a series of leisurely walking tours and some further afield excursions, you will get in-depth information on all buildings, statues, parks, markets, places of worship and any other point of interest, researched through personal visits and by drawing on the expertise of locals. Every step of the way, uncluttered easy-to-follow maps guide you around the city.

This book is organised in a number of easily digestible chunks:

- ***Getting to know Baku*** gives a brief history of the city and examines its history, geography and demographics.
- ***Part 1*** takes you on a walking tour around the main sights of Baku's old city.
- ***Part 2*** explores the nineteenth century oil baron mansions in the boom town.
- ***Part 3*** visits the stunning parks perched on the highest slopes of Baku.
- ***Part 4*** takes a stroll along the beautiful corniche running next to the Caspian Sea and then indulges in

some retail therapy.

- *Part 5* goes further afield to take in the sights of Baku's suburbs and further afield.
- *Part 6* gives you all the essential practical information needed to make your trip plain sailing.

List of Maps

Here are the maps that feature in this guide:

- **Map A**: Double Gates to Maiden tower
- **Map B**: Maiden Tower to the Palace of the Shirvanshahs
- **Map C**: Palace of the Shirvanshahs
- **Map D**: Palace of the Shirvanshahs back to the Double Gates
- **Map E**: Boom Town
- **Map F**: Parks and Panoramas
- **Map G**: Carpet Museum and along Baku Boulevard
- **Map H**: Baku Boulevard to Fountain Square
- **Map I**: Ateshgah Fire Temple
- **Map J**: Yanar Dag
- **Map K**: Heydar Aliyev Centre
- **Map L**: Gobustan National Park

Getting to know Baku

A brief history

A hundred thousand years ago, the semi-arid land around modern-day Baku was instead grassy savanna with a wealth of animal and plant life. It is natural that humans would have been present to some extent, and indeed some traces of habitation have been found from the Stone Age. Moving forward into the Bronze age, the evidence that there was a settlement where Baku now sits grows stronger and includes rock carvings in the area now home to Baku's Bayil suburb, and an astronomical observatory in Nardarn to the city's north. In the first century AD, the Romans reached this part of the world, and today's village of Ramana appears on their maps. There is a shortage of information about the Baku area during the following centuries, although the fifth-century Greek historian Priscus did mention the "Bakuvian fires" emanating from the ground.

The region eventually became known as Shirvan, and from the mid-ninth century was ruled by the Shirvanshahs (literally "Kings of Shirvan"). They were destined to reign until the sixteenth century, although during this time

Shirvan's independence was punctuated by long periods of subordination by other neighbouring powers, reducing it to a vassal state.

The twelfth century was a period of relative stability, and the Shirvanshahs were able to set about building strong defences, including the fortifications surrounding the old city of Baku and the Maiden Tower, to resist their many foreign enemies. Nevertheless, Baku and Shirvan were overrun by the Mongols in 1235, which ushered in two brutal centuries of Mongol, and then Timurid, subordination.

The fortunes of the Shirvan state were revived in the fifteenth century when Shirvanshah Ibrahim I succeeded in repelling the foreign oppressors. Together with his successors, Khalilullah I and Farrukh Yassar, the Shirvanshahs then oversaw a period of renaissance, during which the Palace of the Shirvanshahs was built. However, this was not to last, and in 1501 Shirvan and Baku was invaded by Safavid King Ismail I, whose forces ransacked the city and even exhumed the bodies from the Shirvanshah mausoleum. While Shirvan managed to limp along as a vassal state for a few more years, Ismail I's son, Tahmasp I, fully incorporated it into the Safavid empire in 1538, putting an end once and for all to the Shirvanshah reign.

Safavid rule lasted for the next two centuries until 1722 when Russian and Ottoman forces invaded Baku. For the rest of the eighteenth century, this heralded varying degrees of Russian influence, Shirvan independence and conflicts between Russian and Persian armies. At the very end of the century, Russia began a concerted effort to conquer the Caucasus once and for all, and Baku was captured and fully integrated into the Russian Empire by 1813.

In 1846 the world's first oil well was drilled in the Bibi-Heybat suburb of Baku, marking the start of the oil boom. A period of frenzied development followed for the rest of the nineteenth century, and well into the twentieth, which saw the city rapidly expand from its old core. Many palatial mansions, civic amenities, parks and boulevards were built during this time by magnates such as Musa Naigiyev, Murtuza Mukhtarov and Shamsi Asadullayev. By World War I, Baku was producing 15% of the entire world's oil output.

After the collapse of the Russian Empire in 1918, independence was declared and the short-lived "Azerbaijan Democratic Republic" was founded. However, in April 1920 the Russian Red Army crossed the border, captured Baku the next day, and went on to occupy the whole country. The city then became the capital of the "Azerbaijan Soviet Socialist Republic".

The wait to become independent again was to last for more than seventy years. In 1991, following the collapse of the USSR, the Azerbaijani flag flew once more over a free country. Baku has now become the vibrant beating heart of Azerbaijan, and the centre for science, culture, politics and industry.

Geography

Baku is Azerbaijan's capital and the largest city in the Caucasus. It is situated in the extreme east of Azerbaijan on the Absheron peninsula, which juts out into the waters of the Caspian Sea, and lies just above 40 degrees north. A surprising geographical anomaly is that much of Baku sits well under sea level, at -28 m, making it the world's lowest capital city. Its more famous counterpart, Amsterdam, is a mere 2 m below sea level.

Like the pearl in an oyster, the heart of the city is the compact old town or "Icherisheher" in Azerbaijani. Inside its ancient walls, the streets are narrow and winding and there is a merciful absence of traffic. Spreading out from the old town away from the sea is a band of development created during the nineteenth-century oil boom when money flooded in and Baku outgrew the confines of the old city walls. This area has broad boulevards, leafy parks and lavish mansions. Spreading out once more from this "Boom Town" is the modern-day city which started to grow up during Soviet times, with roads laid out on a more rigid grid pattern. The outlying suburbs are home to heavy industry, oil extraction and quarries.

Leading the city's main thoroughfares is the ever-busy Neftchilar Prospect which runs parallel to the Caspian Sea shoreline. The road begins at Baku Crystal Hall in the south, runs past the old city and Government House, before changing its name to Nobel Prospect and heading out across the Absheron Peninsula. Azadliq Prospect runs north across the entire city from Government House, past 28 May Station and beyond. Finally, from Nizami Park, near the Double Gates of the Old Town, the Zerbaycan Prospect eventually passes the bus station and 20 January metro before splitting into the M1 and M4 national motorways.

Demographics

Just over 2.3 million people live in Baku, which means that a quarter of the entire Azerbaijan population lives within its municipal limits. While in Soviet times there were sizeable Russian and Armenian populations, Baku today is less cosmopolitan with the city comprising more than 90% native Azerbaijanis.

The majority of people follow Shia Islam. However, Azerbaijan is a secular state and conserves religious freedom. Accordingly, you can find synagogues and a wide variety of churches serving Christian minorities.

Languages

Azerbaijani is the official language, a Turkic language closely related and partially mutually intelligible with modern day Turkish. It is the native tongue of 92.5% of Azerbaijanis. Half of the population is monolingual, and among those speaking other languages, English and Russian are the most popular. In the Nagorno-Karabakh enclave Armenian is spoken, although this area is not under government control.

PART 1 - Old Town (Icherisheher)

All of Baku used to be contained with the walls of the present-day old town, and it was only in the mid-nineteenth century, with the advent of the oil industry, that the city eventually expanded beyond the walls and then kept on growing. It was at this time that the area within the walls became aptly known as "Icherisheher", which is Azerbaijani for "Inner City".

Icherisheher was built in the middle ages, and the twelfth century saw the erection of the Maiden Tower and a surge in construction within the city walls. The old town comprised a maze of winding streets, which can still be seen today, dividing it into nine separate districts. These neighbourhoods were centred on a mosque, many of which still stand such as the Juma, Siniqqala, Mohammed and Shah mosques, each with a mullah.

Every merchant and artisan had a shop and many of these clustered together in a great bazaar stretching from Juma mosque to the Maiden Tower. Buyers and suppliers came from all over Azerbaijan, and from Persia, Russia and Central Asia. To cater to the needs of all these visitors, and residents, many lavish caravanserais and bathhouses were built. Then in the relative stability of the fifteenth-century, the

Shirvanshah rulers built their palace on high ground overlooking the entire city.

Many of these mosques, caravanserais, bathhouses, bazaars, walls and towers are well preserved, making Icherisheher a living history book. This walking tour, split into manageable chunks, takes in all the highlights.

— Double Gates to Maiden Tower —

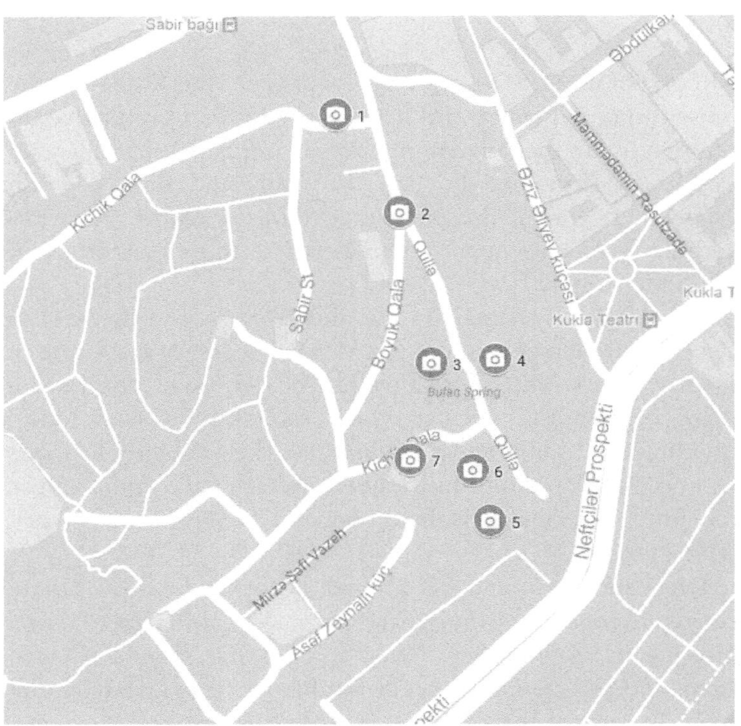

Map A | Double Gates to Maiden Tower

* * *

Double Gate (Qosa Qala Qapisi)

Construction of Baku's old city walls started as far back as the twelfth century. A plaque in Arabic script was uncovered during restoration work, detailing that the wall was '... ordered by the glorious, wise, just, victorious, ruling monarch, supporter of Islam and of Muslims, the great Shirvanshah Abdul Khoja Manujohr.' This ruler was on the throne from 1120 to 1149, nicely pinpointing the construction date.

Today, 500 m of Baku's old city walls remain standing, and the most impressive feature of this stretch of monumental masonry is the Double Gate, or Qosa Qala Qapisi *(Map A, Point 1)*. This portal connects the ancient city with the more recent nineteenth-century neighbourhood built during the oil boom years.

In bas-relief above each of the gates is the ancient coat of arms of Baku, showing two lions either side of a bull's head, along with a representation of the sun and moon. In the seventeenth century, the German explorer Kaempfer tried to decipher the meaning of this coat of arms with local historians. He determined that the bull represents the city of Baku itself, as in ancient times the land could not adequately support crops and locals turned to cattle farming instead. The flanking lions protect the bull, or city, and so represent the walls themselves. The moon and sun show that this protection is unwavering, and continues both during the day and at night.

Museum of Archaeology and Ethnography

Once you have passed through the Double Gates, you are in

the Old Town proper. Walking straight down the cobbled street, you will see many buildings with the distinctive architectural feature of balconies hanging over the road. Carpet sellers are everywhere. Eventually, the road forks and the Museum of Ethnography and Archaeology *(Map A, Point 2)* is located at this junction.

The archaeological display at the museum covers Azerbaijani history from the Stone Age through to the Middle Ages. Artefacts show how these early people lived, and sheds light on their art, lifestyle, culture and values. The focus of the ethnographic section is on more recent times and looks at life during the nineteenth and twentieth centuries.

The museum is open weekdays between 10 am and 5 pm. It is closed on Saturdays and Sundays.

Caravanserais

Back at the junction outside the museum, take the left-hand fork. This narrow street leads to two facing caravanserais. These provided weary travellers with accommodation, and also somewhere to eat, feed their horses, camels and mules, hire temporary guards and meet new trading partners. All caravanserais are designed for safety and security; any potential assailants are hindered by just one entrance and windows only facing the interior courtyard.

On the right-hand side of the street is the fifteenth-century Bukhara Caravanserai *(Map A, Point 3)*, so called because traders from modern-day Uzbekistan built it. Initially used by Central Asian merchants, this square building has cells arrayed along each wall, facing inwards into a calm, octagonal courtyard.

On the left, the fourteenth-century Multani Caravanserai *(Map A, Point 4)* takes its name from the Pakistani city

Multan, established by visitors and merchants from the subcontinent. These were possibly the same people involved in the development of the Ateshgah Fire Temple. This caravanserai has a similar construction to the one just across the street. Today, both are fancy restaurants, offering a wide range of Azerbaijani cuisine.

Approaching Maiden Tower

A few steps from the caravanserais will take you out into an open area, behind which the Maiden Tower *(Map A, Point 5)* looms. The area below street level is the excavated remains of a seventeenth-century marketplace *(Map A, Point 6)*. It comprises a large inner courtyard surrounded by an iwan, which is a vaulted, rectangular construction open on one side. In the market are displays of tombstones, sarcophagi and carvings that were found in Baku and across the Absheron peninsula.

Next to the marketplace is the distinctive dome-roofed Hadji Bani bathhouse *(Map A, Point 7)*, built in the late fifteenth-century. The bathhouse had remained undiscovered until archaeological excavations in the 1960s. Although today we think of bathing as a fundamentally private activity to be conducted in the sanctuary of our bathroom, in the Middle Ages they played a vital public role. They promoted health and hygiene and were also a place where people could go to relax and unwind. The Old Town of Baku has many bathhouses, often situated close to caravanserais. After a long, tiring journey along one of the many Silk Roads, the bathhouse represented a very welcome luxury, and one not to be missed.

* * *

— Maiden Tower (Qiz Qalasi) —

The imposing and ancient Maiden Tower looms over the Old Town and is the iconic landmark of Baku. While Paris has the Eiffel Tower and London Big Ben, this structure represents Baku. Maiden Tower became a UNESCO World Heritage Site due to its historical significance, and today graces the 10 Manat banknote and 5 Gepik coin.

The tower is a cylinder, just shy of 30 m high and with a diameter of 16.5 m. Inside there are eight floors, linked by a winding stone staircase. A buttress, the same height of the tower, sticks out of the tower on the seaward side. The solidity of construction is staggering, and the tower is built on a massive slab of rock, with foundations extending down 14 m. The walls at the base are 5 m thick and contain an ingenious drainage system designed to carry sewerage and wastewater from each of the floors.

These are all concrete facts. So far so good. But now the confusion begins. There are many conflicting theories regarding the history of the tower, its purpose, its date of construction and just about everything else. To borrow a quote from Winston Churchill, the tower is "a riddle, wrapped in a mystery, inside an enigma".

An impressive museum is arranged over the internal floors, with each level examining the conflicting theories and attempting to peel back some of these layers of mystery. As you climb upwards you will eventually reach the flat roof of the tower, from where you get a 360-degree panoramic view of Baku's Old Town, Boom Town, Flame Towers, Corniche and the glittering Caspian Sea.

There have been a few reconstructions of the tower in the past decades. During the most recent of these, from 2009-13, the stone walls were extensively renovated. Interestingly, the nooks and crannies between these stones were home to common swifts. The archaeologists did not want to make these birds homeless, so they built small replacement nests on the walls of the neighbouring buildings. So when wandering around the area of the tower, keep your eyes open, and you may see some of the swifts flying in and out of their new homes!

Theories abound

There are no surviving written sources which document the construction or purpose of the tower and, accordingly, scientists, architects, historians and academics have come up with a mind-boggling range of theories. However, these theories coalesce into four primary schools of thought.

The first of these theoretical conclusions is that the tower was a Zoroastrian temple dedicated to ancient pre-Islamic Persian goddesses Mitra and Anahita. In the mid-1980s, local Azeri researchers Davud Akhundov and Hassan Hassanov found archaeological evidence showing that there were purportedly seven fire exits on the top of the structure. Supporting this theory of religious and ritual use is the shape of the tower when seen from above. It resembles a teardrop, or number 6 or 9, depending on one's viewpoint. This shape is known as the buta, a symbol of the fire and light that is important in Zoroastrianism. The Paisley pattern so familiar in modern-day clothing design derives from the buta, and this motif is found in many other artistic applications in old Baku. Today, fires still burn on the roof during the Persian new year Nowruz celebrations, a festival which has strong links to Zoroastrianism.

Other scholars believe that the tower had a more practical defensive purpose. A secret tunnel linking the Palace of the Shirvanshahs to the Maiden Tower lends credence to this theory, as does the integral well in the centre of the structure which would allow people within the tower to get fresh water while under siege. However, academics supporting the defence-related theory divide into two camps of thought. The first set of scholars believe that the tower dates to around the twelfth century, the same time the Old Town's defensive walls were built. The second group put forward the theory that the tower was built as a stand-alone structure much earlier in the fifth or sixth century. They have identified similarities with other similarly-aged castles and towers part of the northern Persian empire defensive network. They also point to differences in the stone used to construct the tower than that used in the adjacent city walls.

A final theory states that the tower was an astronomical observatory. An Azeri archaeologist, Gara Ahmadov, claims that the thirty stone projections on the bottom part of the tower, and a further thrity-one stone markers on the upper part, are related to the days of the month. While this opinion is widely discredited, there is still little evidence to support the other theories, and so cannot be wholly ruled out.

Legends

Many legends swirl around the tower, as you'd expect for something that has stood so prominently in Baku for well over a thousand years. The most widely told legend is that of a king who fell in love with his daughter and decided to marry her. Understandably the daughter did not particularly welcome this prospect, so she attempted to delay the marriage by asking her father to build the loftiest tower possible. His passion was such that he did just that, and the result was the tower you see today. The daughter then climbed the stairs, telling her father she was going to admire the view, but instead threw herself off and crashed onto the rocks far below. This tale, in many varying forms, is still told in Azeris plays and poetry. The national ballet troupe even performs it, and while in Baku you may be lucky enough to see it staged.

So according to this legend the name Maiden Tower makes sense. However, as with everything else concerning this structure, there are differences of opinion regarding its nomenclature. Some believe 'maiden' refers to the towers' impregnability. Others think that maiden, 'qiz' in Azerbaijani, refers to the water goddess Anahita that features in the Avesta, the Zoroastrian holy book. Whatever the truth, the Maiden Tower does not look likely to reveal any of its secrets any time soon.

— Maiden Tower to the Palace of the Shirvanshahs —

* * *

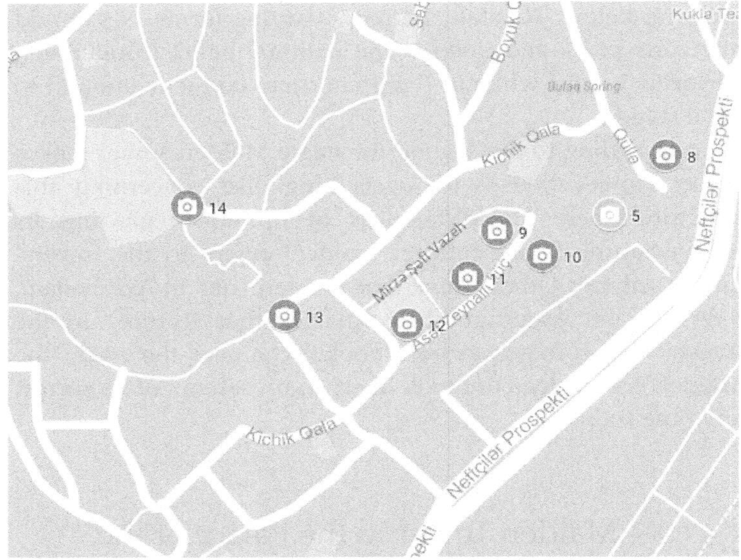

Map B | Maiden Tower to the Palace of the Shirvanshahs

Before you set off for the other jewel of the Old Town, the Palace of the Shirvanshahs, take a moment to walk around to the side of the Maiden Tower that faces the Caspian Sea. As you look at the tower, you will see an ornate building to its right. This is the Hajinski Mansion *(Map B, Point 8)*.

Hajinski Mansion

This prominent neighbour of the Maiden Tower was built in 1912 for the wealthy local oil baron Isa Bey Hajinski, and was at that time one of the tallest buildings in the city. There are many art nouveau flourishes, comic faces carved into the limestone of the building, and mosaics in the style of ancient Assyria. Seven individually-design spires and balconies in a variety of styles adorn this majestic building. The building's aim was to communicate the power and status of its owner, and it undoubtedly achieves this goal.

However, there is a distinct lack of harmony between the various building facades. As an explanation, it is alleged that the architect funnelled funds materials into the construction of his own lavish house, although there are indications that this was standard practice during this period.

Hajinski died in 1918, just after the Russian revolution. During the Soviet time, the building was split up into different apartments, often used by visiting dignitaries, the most famous of whom was General Charles de Gaulle in 1944. Another celebrated resident was Yusif Mammadaliyev, an outstanding Azerbaijani chemist and twice President of the National Academy of Sciences.

In 2007 the facades of the building were comprehensively renovated. Nowadays the ground floor is home to the stores of exclusive brands, such as Tiffany, Bvlgari and Christian Dior.

Go back up towards the other side of Maiden tower. Turn left, and you will be at the beginning of Asaf Zeynalli Street. This thoroughfare takes its name from the accomplished Azerbaijani composer, who wrote many symphonies and folk songs before his untimely death aged 23. The leading music school of Azerbaijan is also named after him.

Along this street are many buildings of note.

Madrasa Mosque

Diagonally across the plaza fronting the Maiden Tower is the tiny Madrasa Mosque *(Map B, Point 9)*, dating to the twelfth century. Its shape is an almost perfect cube topped out with a small dome, and has no minarets. The name 'Madrasa' derives from the Arabic word for school, and in this building mullahs taught students the Qur'an, natural sciences, mathematics and eastern languages, and also trained aspiring secondary school teachers.

These days the building is inhabited by carpet and souvenir sellers.

Mugham Club

Opposite the Madrasa Mosque is the Mugam Club *(Map B, Point 10)*, a restaurant housed in an old and picturesque caravanserai. Its two-storey wings enclose a pleasant courtyard containing tables interspersed with small trees and fountains. If you're passing by at lunch or dinner time, it's a great place to try out some Azerbaijani food, and in the evening there are traditional music and dance performances.

Ashur (Lezgi) Mosque

A few steps down A. Zeynalli Street, on the right-hand side, is the Ashur Mosque *(Map B, Point 11)*, which takes its name from the twelfth-century architect Najaf Ashur Ibrahim. In the nineteenth century, the mosque became known informally as the Lezgi mosque. During that time many men from Dagestan, Russia, came to Baku to work in the oil boom. These were mostly of the Lezgin ethnic group, and as they prayed mainly at this mosque, the name entered public etymology. Inside there is a single prayer hall.

The shape of the mosque is parallelepiped, or in other words a slightly elongated cube. Some academics believe that this twelfth-century building sits over a much earlier fire-worshipping temple. Archaeological investigations are still ongoing, and in the future yet more of this site's long history may be unearthed.

Juma (Friday) Mosque

A short distance further down A. Zeynalli Street, on the same side, is the Juma, or Friday, Mosque *(Map B, Point 12)*. The entrance to the mosque is a beautifully and intricately carved portal, replete with geometric and floral designs and Arabic calligraphy. This site has had a long and eventful history, and as with the Ashur mosque, archaeologists suggest that the Juma mosque was originally built over a Zoroastrian fire-worshipping temple in the twelfth century. The minaret, built in 1437 by Shirvan Shah Khalilullah I, is decorated with elaborate stalactite carvings (muqarnas), a common architectural feature found in mosques across Iran. The mosque itself has been rebuilt several times over the centuries, and the philanthropy of the merchant Haji Shikhladi Dadashov in 1899 paid for the construction of the present structure.

Inside, four stout columns in the square prayer hall support a single dome covered in ornate tilework reminiscent of that found in noteworthy Persian buildings in modern-day Iran.

Mohammed Mosque

Turn right after the Juma Mosque, and at the end of the street turn left. After a few steps, you will see the imposing bulk of the minaret of the Muhammed Mosque *(Map B, Point 13)*, one of the oldest buildings in the whole of the Old Town, built in 1078-1079.

The mosque also goes by the name Synyk Gala, roughly translated as 'damaged tower'. This second name came about during the Russo-Persian War in the eighteenth century. Russian warships bombarded Baku, and a shell hit the minaret. Soon after, a storm blew the ships far out to sea, and the inhabitants of Baku took this as a sign of divine retribution. The damaged minaret was eventually repaired in the mid-nineteenth century.

Retrace your steps back along the road outside the mosque, and go straight. Then take the first left and walk uphill. After a meandering 200 m or so you will reach the back of the Palace of the Shirvanshahs. Located on this back wall is the magnificent Murad's Gate *(Map B, Point 14)*.

Murad's Gate

The gate was built much later than the rest of the palace in 1585. At this time, the Ottomans were at war with the neighbouring Safavid Persian Empire, and as part of this campaign, the Turks captured Baku. Accordingly, the gate was named to honour the victorious Sultan of the Ottoman Empire, Murad III.

A celebrated Persian architect from Tabriz designed the gate. The uppermost part of the gate has an Arabic inscription, which states that 'this noble building was built in the days of rule of the most just and the greatest sultan Murad Ulu Rajab-baba Bakuji in the year 994 (1585). Either side of this are two roundels with floral motifs. The semi-dome recess has the stalactites, or muqarnas, popular in Persian architecture at this time. As the gate is much wider than other entrances, this could have been a portal into a building that was either subsequently demolished or not built at all.

From Murad's Gate, walk along the road that follows the palace walls. Eventually, you will emerge at the front entrance of the palace. The ticket office is here.

— Palace of the Shirvanshahs —

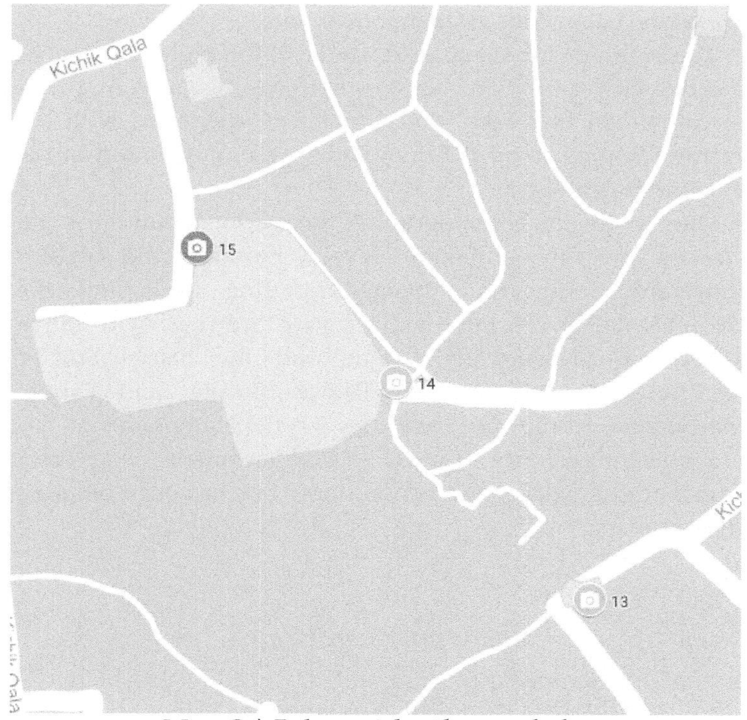

Map C | Palace of the Shirvanshahs

The Palace of the Shirvanshahs *(Map C, Point 15)* is undoubtedly one of the two gems of Baku, the other being the Maiden Tower, and a visit here should be on the top of every visitor's list. Shah Khalilullah I began construction in the early fifteenth century when he moved the capital of the Shirvan state from Shamakhy to Baku. The name Shirvanshahs translates into English as 'Kings of the Shirvan'. The complex is now regarded as being the finest example of Shirvan architecture and is designated a UNESCO World Heritage Site. It's importance to the nation is undeniable, and graces the back of the 10 Manat banknote.

The entire palace complex is at one of the highest points of the old city, and there are far-reaching views from many places. When first built, the palace was integrated with the surrounding city, and the high walls were only added in the nineteenth century.

Due to the local topography, the various buildings are arrayed on three different levels. Fronting the highest courtyard is the main palace building itself and the Divankhana. In the intermediary yard are the Seyid Yahya Mausoleum, Keygubad Mosque and the Baiolv Stones. Slightly lower again is the Palace Mosque and Family Mausoleum. At the very lowest level is the Hammam.

Eighteenth-century naval bombardments severely damaged the palace, and restoration work has been ongoing since then.

The Upper Courtyard

Once past the ticket counter, you enter the upper courtyard, bordered on three sides by palace buildings with the fourth offering expansive views over Baku towards the Flame Towers. As you walk towards the entrance to the Palace building, you will notice many dozens of bullet holes peppering the stone walls, visible reminders of the Armenian-Azeri conflict of 1918.

Main palace building

The palace itself dates back to the early fifteenth century, 1411 to be precise, and its construction was ordered by Shirvanshah Sheyyk Ibrahim I. It has a total of 52 rooms arrayed over two floors connected by three narrow winding stairways. The King and the royal family used the upper part, and so the steps in the main arched entranceway go all the way up to that floor. The lower level was for servants and household staff.

One of the most impressive rooms is the Throne Hall, which acted as a focal point for palace life and state events. An idea of its previous glory is given by the fifteenth-century court poet, Badr Shirvani, who wrote: "It is blue as the sky and golden as the sun here. When light passes through the windows to fall upon the ceiling full of decorative designs, the stars shine from within the blue glow of the dome". Indeed, archaeologists have found evidence that blue tiles adorned the interior of the palace. Another highlight is the Banquet Hall, and you should look out for the windows covered in geometric stone latticework, through which you can glimpse lovely views of the Caspian Sea.

Today, artefacts and relics from throughout the palace's long history are displayed in many of the palace rooms. However, due to looting and bombardments during the sixteenth to eighteenth centuries by Russian and Ottoman forces, most items on display are from the last two hundred years or so. Nonetheless, there are many fascinating and beautiful artefacts from swords, musical instruments and clothing through to household objects, carpets and jewellery.

Divankhana

Back out in the upper courtyard, walk through a small doorway in the northern wall to see the Divankhana, regarded as the most exceptional examples of medieval architecture anywhere in the Middle East.

The Divankhana is a small octagonal pavilion, surrounded by an open balcony edged with columns and arches, on a raised platform. This construction is in the centre of a courtyard surrounded by a gallery-arcade with similarly-shaped columns and arches.

The main entrance is particularly ornate. There are striking floral motifs representing fig and vine leaves, plants common throughout Azerbaijan. Stalactites or muqarnas support a fluted semi-cupola. Either side of the entrance are two hexagonal inscriptions, the left reading "There is no God but Allah" and "Prophet Mohammed is the messenger of Allah", and the right repeating "Allah is single" and "Mohammed" six times each. Once you walk through this portal, you enter a vestibule with yet more floral carvings and Arabic calligraphy, before reaching the pavilion itself.

There is still much debate regarding the use of this building. Some scholars believe that it was a royal courthouse, others think that it was used for receiving visiting delegations, while yet more see evidence that it was a royal tomb for Farrukh Yassar.

Walk back into the upper courtyard, and walk straight across to find the staircase leading to the middle and lower courtyards.

The Middle Courtyard

* * *

The Mausoleum of Seyid Yahya

Seyid Yahya was a royal scholar and astronomer in the court of Khalilullah I. His mausoleum is situated in a separate, slightly sunken courtyard, and is octagonally-shaped with a distinctive 7.5 m high pyramidal roof. It resembles tombs found in the medieval Seljuk Turko-Persian empire.

The mausoleum comprises a lower subterranean part containing the tomb itself, and an upper portion used for religious ceremonies. The building is attached to the oldest part of the palace, the Keygubad Mosque, which is now in ruins.

The Bailov Stones

Displayed around the external walls of the middle courtyard are the thirteenth-century Bailov Stones. All these come from Sabayil Fortress, which was built on a small island 300 m out in the Caspian Sea.

This fortress was a substantial structure, more than 175 m long and 35 m wide, with two-metre thick walls, three circular and twelve semi-circular towers. A scale model in one of the rooms of the main palace building shows the Sabayil Fortress as it would have been in its prime.

However, the building did not last long. In 1306 there was a cataclysmic earthquake in the Caspian Sea which not only caused the castle to crumble but also led to the sea level dramatically rising. The ruins were submerged, in effect becoming Azerbaijan's very own Atlantis, which was not rediscovered until the eighteenth century when water levels dropped again. Today you can still see its outline from the top of the Maiden Tower.

In 1939, an archaeological expedition found more than 700 inscribed stones, some of which now reside in this courtyard. These formed a frieze that completely encircled the castle walls. Humans and animals such as horses and camels embellish the letters on these stones, and it is rare to see such examples of Arabic inscriptions in an anthropomorphic style. Historians analysing them have found the names of fifteen individual Shirvanshahs and other valuable historical information from that time.

The Lower Courtyard

A wall separates the lower courtyard from the other sections of the palace. Here there are two buildings, the Palace Mosque and the Shirvanshah's Mausoleum.

Palace Mosque

This mosque was built in the mid-fifteenth century, and an inscription around the 22 m high minaret confirms this, stating that "The Great Sultan Khalilullah I order the erection of this minaret. May God preserve his rule as Shah. Year 845". That year in the Islamic calendar corresponds to 1441-42 in the Gregorian calendar.

The central part of the mosque consists of a square domed prayer hall, with a smaller adjacent hall for women. Upon entry, you can see the Mihrab on the facing wall, which indicates the direction of Mecca and acts as a kind of doorway to the holy city. In the upper corners of the mosque, and around the lower part of the dome, the necks of large jars protrude from the stonework. These were added to enhance the acoustics of the prayer hall.

The Mausoleum of the Shirvanshahs

The royal family's mausoleum is a rectangular-shaped building topped with an octagonal dome decorated with stars. Many years ago, these stars would have been filled in with blue tiles. The grand entrance to the building has many of the features seen in other portals in the palace, including floral carvings, stalactites and a concave semi-cupola. The inscription above the door indicates the purpose of the building, saying that "Khalilullah I…ordered to construct this light burial vault for his mother and son in 839" (1435-36). The two tear-drop shaped inscriptions either side of the portal show the architect's name, Memar Ali, along with the words God and Mohammed.

The court poet, Badr Shirvani, again helps us to shed some light on the use of the mausoleum. He recorded that the tomb houses the graces of Khalilullah I himself, his mother, four sons, a cousin and the army commander.

The mausoleum has had a violent past, however, and it was not the peaceful resting place as initially intended. In 1500, the Safavids invaded Baku, and they went about vandalising all of the graves in the mausoleum. It eventually turned out that it was only the tombstones that were destroyed, and the graves underneath escaped without damage.

The Lowest Courtyard

Excavations of the former palace bathhouse

The remains of the seventeenth-century palace bathhouse are on the lowest level of the royal complex and were only discovered in 1939. This hammam was built almost entirely underground to preserve warmth in the winter and to keep it cool in summer months, and only the cupolas poked above ground. The complex had a total of 26 rooms, and the king had his own personal bathroom.

The water came from a reservoir located behind the palace walls, and was heated in a boiler room and then distributed throughout the bathing rooms. Steam was also used to heat the rooms through an underfloor system.

The palace is open daily, 10 am - 6 pm.

— Palace of the Shirvanshahs back to the Double Gates —

Map D | Palace of the Shirvanshahs back to the Double Gates

Once you have finished your visit to the Palace of the

Shirvanshahs, turn left from the main entrance. Follow the road down the slight incline and around the bend. On the right-hand side is the Museum of Miniature Books *(Map D, Point 16).*

Museum of Miniature Books

This unique museum, supposedly the only one of its kind in the world, opened its doors in 2002. Its founder, Zarifa Salahova, is the daughter of the decorated Azerbaijani artist Tahir Salahov, and over the years she has built a collection of 6,500 books.

On display are many tiny volumes from distinguished Azerbaijaini and Soviet authors, as well as the works of the giants of Western literature such as Shakespeare, Hemingway and Conan Doyle. The oldest piece on display is a seventeenth-century Qur'an.

A highlight of the collection, and the most extreme example of miniaturisation are three of the world's tiniest books, each measuring just 2 mm by 2 mm. To read them a powerful magnifying glass is required.

The museum is open Tuesdays to Sundays from 10 am to 5 pm, and entrance is free.

Old walls

From the museum, retrace your steps back past the Palace of the Shirvanshahs and head straight, until you reach the old city walls *(Map D, Point 17),* then turn right. You can then follow these walls all the way back to the Double Gates. On the way, there are opportunities to walk along a path at the top of the walls, and there are various canons and siege-weapons to admire, such as a fearsome giant catapult.

Quadrangular tower

A short walk along the twelfth-century walls you will encounter a much taller and heavily fortified quadrangular tower *(Map D, Point 18)*, also known as the Donjon. 18 m high and with 2 m thick walls, this tower was used throughout the Middle Ages as an armoury and as a powerful defensive feature. Inside, a spiral staircase links four floors.

There is some debate regarding the tower's age. Some believe that it was built at the same time as the adjoining walls. However, others point to accounts written by the court poet, Badr Shirvani, who specifically noted its construction in 1428-29.

Archaeological excavations in the tower have unearthed quite complex architectural features such as an integral well and a sanitation and ventilation system.

Back to the Double Gates

From the quadrangular tower, continue to follow the street, Kichik Qala, until the T-junction. At this point, turn left, and you will find yourself back at the Double Gates, where this walking tour ends.

PART 2 - Boom Town

In the nineteenth century, Baku was at the very heart of the global oil trade. Forget Saudi Arabia and the Gulf states, Azerbaijan produced well over half of the world's entire oil. As you'd expect, this resulted in rivers of hard currency flowing rapidly into the region. Baku boomed accordingly, and between 1850 and the turn of the century its population exploded, growing faster than London or New York.

Many people grew incredibly rich overnight, and a new oil baron class wanted to show off their wealth. They built hundreds of luxurious mansions, designed by some of the best architects and using architectural styles from all over the world. New avenues were laid out to accommodate this upsurge in construction, and oil baron money supported the creation of new public parks and gardens, concert halls, libraries and theatres.

As the old city was already full, this development rippled outwards from the ancient walls. It created a new cityscape that would have been worthy of London, Paris or any other global city. However, the boom time was destined not to last forever, and in 1920 the Bolsheviks took power in Baku. All this opulent private property was seized and converted into many different apartments for the masses. The oil barons fled as fast as they could.

The good news is that much of this boom time architecture survived the Soviet period, and this walking tour looks at some of the best survivors of that time.

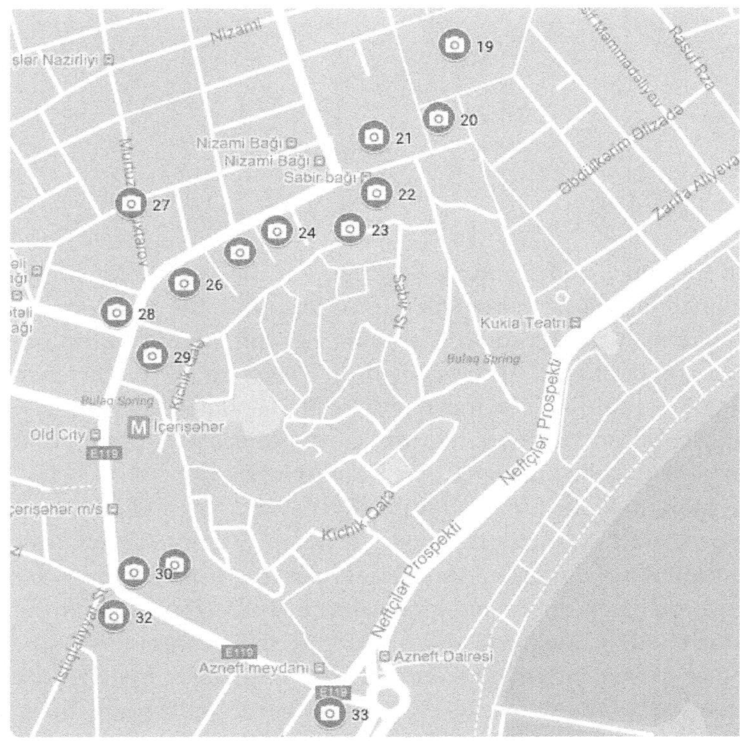

Map E | Boom Town

Fountain Square

This walking tour begins in the leafy surroundings of Fountain Square *(Map E, Point 19)*, built in the mid-nineteenth century. In Soviet times this expansive public space was named after the revolutionary socialist Karl Marx, however, following the construction of many fountains during the 1980s, and independence in 1991, it became popularly known as Fountain Square.

Today this area is a favourite meeting place, particularly after work and at the weekends, and draws its fair share of tourists too. Shops, restaurants and cafes surround the square. Keep your eyes open for two charming modern statues depicting typical Baku residents. The one outside McDonald's shows a young woman on a mobile phone sheltering under an umbrella, and another next to a fountain shows another young lady this time busy putting on her lipstick. You won't be able to miss them as there is a steady stream of people taking selfies with them.

Nizami Museum of Literature

Exit the square in the southwestern corner where you see a two-storey KFC, and you will find the grand Nizami Museum of Literature *(Map E, Point 20)* on your left. This institution preserves and showcases the literature of Azerbaijan. Even before entering this museum, you get a sense of the pride in the country's literary heroes. The magnificent facade of this museum features six imposing statues of the most accomplished Azerbaijani writers and poets, housed in monumental alcoves. The statues show Fizuli, Vagif, Akhundov, Natavan, Mammadguluzade and Jabbarli. The museum takes its name from the most honoured national poet, Nizami Ganjavi. Born in Azerbaijan during the twelfth century, Nizami is considered to be the greatest poet in Persian literature. In addition to having national treasure status in his home country, poetry lovers across Iran, Afghanistan, Kurdistan and Tajikistan revere him.

The building has had a chequered history. It was initially built as a one-storey caravanserai in 1850. Later, at the height of the oil boom, one of the new millionaires, Haji Hajagha Dadashov, purchased the caravanserai, adding a second floor and banqueting room to create the much grander and luxurious Metropol Hotel. Its life in the hospitality was shortlived, however, thanks to the Bolsheviks and for the next couple of decades was occupied by the Trade Union Committee of Azerbaijan. In 1939, on the 800th birthday of Nizami, the government decided to convert the building into a Museum of Literature. Work began, and in 1943 the facade was redesigned to include the six statues you see today. In 1945 the museum's doors opened.

Nizami Park and Monument

Directly across the street from the main facade of the Nizam Museum of Literature, is the Nizami Park *(Map E, Point 21)*. A grand staircase, flanked by willow trees, leads up the slight hill, to a statue of Nizami himself. It was installed at this spot in 1949, created by the People's Artist of Azerbaijan, Fuad Abdurahmanov, a renowned sculptor responsible for many monumental statues around Baku. If you look back towards the Museum of Literature, the statue of Fizuli was also a work by Abdurahmanov.

This statue of Nizami is 6 m high and made from bronze. It stands on an octagonal red granite pedestal, each side of which has bronze plates showing scenes from some of Nizami's most famous works.

Sabir Park and Monument

* * *

When facing the Nizami monument, turn to your left, cross the street, and you'll be in Sabir Park *(Map E, Point 22)*. The focal point of this green space nestling under the old city walls is a statue of the Azerbaijani satirical poet and philosopher, Mirza Alakbar Sabir (1862-1911).

In the first decade of the twentieth century, Sabir was at his most productive, writing extensively for satirical publications. He was mainly involved with the Molla Nasraddin magazine, whose publisher was Jalil Mammadguluzade, also one of the six statues on the facade of the Museum of Literature.

Sabir's work was popular with the working classes throughout the country, as his writing exposed the foibles of Tsarist administrators, greedy landowners, backward clergy and the plight of downtrodden women. His poverty resulted in his early death in 1911.

Taghiyev Gate and Old City Walls

The old city walls form an imposing backdrop to Sabir Park. Slightly to the east of the Sabir statue is the beautiful arched Taghiyev Gate *(Map E, Point 23)*, giving direct access to the Old Town. However, not is all as it seems, and this gate is not a twelfth-century portal but one that was built somewhat more recently in 1877 by Haji Zeynalabdin Taghiyev.

Taghiyev was a local merchant who owned some shops which stood where Sabir Park is today. However, he had great difficulty renting these shops out, because they were thought to be too far from the main bazaar in the old city. So Taghiyev asked permission from Baku city council to break through the old city walls at that point, and erect a new gate to create a shortcut. In those days before the advent of cultural conservation and UNESCO, the council agreed, and the portal was built. Taghiyev's businesses duly flourished.

In 1918, there was a battle at this site when the Armenians were trying to capture the Baku. Taghiyev's son led the inner city defenders and successfully managed to repel the invaders.

Ismailiyya Palace

From Sabir Park, walk west along Istiglaliyyat Street. This thoroughfare is one of the oldest and most prestigious in the entire city, with its name meaning 'independence' or 'sovereignty'. Today it is lined with palaces, universities, government offices and upscale shops and restaurants.

The very first building on the left side is one of the grandest and most ornate of the oil baron mansions, the Ismailiyya Palace *(Map E, Point 24)*, built by the wealthy oil magnate, Musa Naghiyev. While he was widely believed to be the most tight-fisted millionnaire in the city, he went on to create this most lavish palace in the Venetian Gothic style. It was designed to commemorate his deceased son, Ismail, and Naghiyev donated it to the Muslim Charity Society in 1913.

During the 1918 conflict with Armenia, the palace suffered significant fire damage and required extensive restoration in the early part of the 1920s. As part of this reconstruction, the original Islamic motifs which featured on the facade were replaced by the then more ideologically correct Soviet stars. Today, the building houses the Presidium of the Academy of Sciences.

The Institute of Manuscripts

* * *

Millionnaire philanthropist Haji Zeynalabdin Taghiyev constructed this grand building *(Map E, Point 25)* at the turn of the twentieth century. Do not confuse this man with the merchant who built the gate in the old city walls by Sabir Park. Over time, there have been five separate individuals of note in Baku with the same name!

This Taghiyev was born into an impoverished family in Baku, and from an early age worked as a bricklayer. He slowly saved up his money, and during the oil boom invested in the oil business. He used his vast profits to build a diversified business empire spanning shipbuilding, energy, forestry, fishing, banking and real estate. In addition to being an astute businessman, he was involved in many civic projects and funded city trams, theatres and water pipelines.

Taghiyev became increasingly concerned about the closed lives of Muslim girls and their lack of education. He sent his daughters to St Petersburg for schooling, but he wanted people with less means to educate their daughters in Baku. This inspired him to construct a dedicated school for Muslim girls at his own expense. The building, which now houses the Institute of Manuscripts, was completed in 1901 and named the Alexandra School for Girls after the Russian Empress and wife of Nicholas II.

In 1920, the invading Bolsheviks commandeered the building into a headquarters for 'worker, peasant and soldier deputies', and after that housed the Supreme Soviet of the Azerbaijan Republic.

Today's institute collects and catalogues old books and manuscripts which hold particular interest to the nation of Azerbaijan, to the broader region and for Islam. Some of its most treasured artefacts are Azerbaijani medical and pharmaceutical-related manuscripts from the twelfth century. The gem of the entire collection is a complete manuscript of

"Khamsa", a poetry collection penned by Nizami, a seventeenth-century copy of the twelfth-century original.

Azerbaijan State University of Economics

The next big edifice along the left side of Istiglaliyyat Street is the Azerbaijan State University of Economics *(Map E, Point 26)*. Founded in 1930, this is one of the largest educational institutions in the whole of the Caucasus with 18,000 students and one thousand teachers split across nine faculties.

The classic Azerbaijani novel, Ali and Nino by Kurban Said, opens in a classroom in this very building.

Wedding Palace

To see another stunning example of an early twentieth-century oil baron's mansion, try to cross the busy Istiglaliyyat Street (there is an underpass further along if this proves too difficult), and make a quick detour up Murtuza Mukhtarov Street to the junction with Ahmed Cavad Street.

Here on the corner, you will see a magnificent French gothic mansion *(Map E, Point 27)* built in 1911 by the oil baron Murtuza Mukhtarov, after whom the street was eventually named. He made the lavish house as a surprise present for his wife, replicating a manor she fell in love with while travelling in France.

A sweet love story, yet one that eventually ended in tragedy. In 1920, when the Bolsheviks invaded Baku, Mukhtarov forbade them to go inside his wife's precious house with their heavy military boots. However, not only did they enter but they did so on horseback. The humiliated oil baron shot three of them before shooting himself. His wife managed to escape to Istanbul.

During Soviet times, as it is today, the building is used for marriage registrations, so the love story still lives on!

Nariman Narimanov Museum

Retrace your steps back down Murtuza Mukhtarov Street to its junction with Istiglaliyyat Street and turn right. After a short block, you will come to the museum dedicated to the life and times of Nariman Narimanov *(Map E, Point 28)*, the Azerbaijani Bolshevik, writer, doctor and statesman.

Born in 1870, Narimanov's early plays and stories focused on highlighting outdated customs, traditions and religious practices, and called for their abandonment. He also stood up for the rights of hard done by local peasants. When the 1905 revolution burst into life, Narimanov immediately joined the Bolshevik party, leading various movements and protests. As a result, the authorities exiled him to Astrakhan for five years. After the 1917 revolution, Narimanov became the leader of the Azerbaijani social democratic party, which was to become the Azerbaijan communist party, and in 1920-21 headed the government of Soviet Azerbaijan.

His importance is undelrined by Leon Tolstoy, who called his death the most significant loss to the eastern world after Lenin. His ashes were given the honour of being interred in the Kremlin walls in Moscow. Today you can see many streets, parks and buildings named after him all over Azerbaijan, and even across Russia.

The museum consists of the four rooms of the apartment in which Narimanov lived from 1913-18. The exhibits comprise documents and materials relating to his early life, political career, writing and family.

* * *

City Hall

Crossing back to the other side of Istiglaliyyat Street, the impressive Baroque building to the right of the university is the Baku City Hall *(Map E, Point 29)*. Three stories with a grand clock tower and red decorative bricks and marble imported from Italy, the City hall contains the residence of the mayor, various other public staterooms and the session hall.

Philharmonic Hall and Fountain Park

Continuing down Istiglaliyyat Street, you will pass the red line Metro station Icherisheher. A few metres further on, on the left-hand side where the street curves around, is the Azerbaijan State Philharmonic Hall *(Map E, Point 30)*.

It was built in 1910-12 in an ornate Italian Renaissance style inspired by the l'Opera de Monte Carlo and is yet another clear example of the effect copious oil dollars had during the boom years. After a renovation in 1993, the building took its name from the famous Azerbaijani composer and conductor, Muslim Magomayev.

The interior is predominantly German Rococo and comprises a Summer Hall with one thousand seats and a Winter Hall seating 610. It is now home to state orchestras, choirs, dance troupes and folk music organisations.

Just behind the Philharmonic Hall is one of Baku's oldest and most beautiful green spaces, the Fountain Park *(Map E, Point 31)*. This has a French baroque fountain, surrounded by an elegant, whitewashed arched colonnade, and is a popular rendezvous point for young couples. Even Ali and Nino met here! There are fantastic views to be had; the old city walls form a dramatic backdrop, the Flame Towers poke their heads above the trees at various points, and the whole park slopes gently down to the sparkling waters of the Caspian Sea. It's a relaxing and peaceful place to pause on any tour around Baku.

National Art Museum of Azerbaijan

Just across Niyazi Street from the Philharmonic Hall is the National Art Museum of Azerbaijan *(Map E, Point 32)*. The museum spreads across two buildings standing next to each other.

The first building, which is on your left side as you view the museum from the street, was originally built as an oil boom mansion for De Bour of Rothschilds, the company that eventually became Shell. Another famous resident of this mansion was the prominent Bolshevik Nariman Narimanov. The second building, just up the hill next to the President's office, was originally a secondary school for Russian girls.

There are sixty rooms in the whole museum, thirty in each building, displaying more than 3000 items. The European collection includes works by a diverse selection of sixteenth to nineteenth century Italian, Flemish, German and Russian painters. The Azerbaijani section features art from the last century from prominent local painters, as well as ancient ceramics and metalwork.

In a small back courtyard there are bullet-ridden statues of the Azerbaijani composer Uzeyir Hajibeyov, singer Bulbul and poet Natavan. These were displayed in the town of Shusha in Nagorno-Karabakh, considered the cultural heartland of Azerbaijan, and were used as target practice by Armenian troops.

The museum is open Tuesdays to Sundays, and the entrance fee is 10 Manat for foreigners and 5 Manat for locals.

SOCAR

From the museum, stroll down Niyazi Street towards the Caspian. At the end of the street, fronting the Neftchilar Prospect, is the vast three-storey oil boom mansion home to SOCAR *(Map E, Point 33)*, the State Oil Company of the Azerbaijan Republic.

The building was built in 1896 and was purchased in the early 1900s by Mir Babayev, a local folk singer, which brings us to another story of how oil can change someone's fortunes overnight. Mir Babeyev was a folk singer with a magnificent voice, who began to be invited to perform at oil baron weddings. At one such event, he so deeply moved the immensely wealthy relatives of the groom that he was given oil-producing land as a lavish gift. Very soon he was producing thousands of barrels of oil and expanded his operation to include three more oil fields and eighteen oil rigs. With his new found wealth he purchased the building which now houses SOCAR. He lived there in splendour until 1920, when he fled the country following the Bolshevik take over.

Today, SOCAR has outgrown the venerable old building and has constructed a massive new skyscraper further out on Heydar Aliyev Avenue. It is the tallest in Azerbaijan and is set to become a brand new landmark for the city, rivalling the Flame Towers.

This is the endpoint of this walking tour.

PART 3 - Parks and Panoramas

Funicular

From the endpoint of the previous walking tour, the SOCAR building, walk south along Neftchilar Prospect, with the Caspian Sea on your left, for about 200 m, and then turn right up Shovkat Alakbarova. The Funicular station *(Map F, Point 34)* will be directly ahead, and the starting point of the next walking tour, Parks and Panoramas.

* * *

Map F: Parks and Panoramas

The Funicular connects Neftchilar Prospect with Dagestu Park and saves a long, steep climb up the hill. The railway track is just under half a kilometre long, and the train leaves approximately every ten minutes throughout the day between 10 am and 10 pm.

The lower station is named Bahram Gur, after the mythical Azerbaijani hero. You can see his statue directly in front of the station in a fountain pool, which depicts the hero using a giant sword to slay a fierce dragon. This character comes from Nizami's poem, "Seven Beauties". The upper station is named Shehidler Xiyabani, the Azerbaijani translation of

"Martyr's Lane" found in Upland Park.

On the journey up the hill, you can get panoramic views of Baku and the Caspian Sea through the train's large windows.

Flame Towers

This trio of skyscrapers *(Map F, Point 35)* is the most prominent landmark of Baku and can be glimpsed from all over the city, forming a futuristic backdrop. When you walk out of the upper Funicular station, you get to see the towers up close.

The buildings, reaching up to a height of 182 m, house apartments, offices, and the luxurious five-star Fairmont Hotel. The long history of fire worship in Baku inspires their design, and from any vantage point, the distinctive curved shapes of the towers appear as three massive flames. They rest on a triangular podium which comprises leisure facilities, restaurants, cafes, cinemas, shops and parking.

More than ten thousand LED lights cover the towers, and at night they turn into massive LED display screens and can be seen from the furthest points of the city.

Between the Funicular station and the Flame Towers is the Shehidlar Khiyabani mosque, and this juxtaposition of the more traditional face of Baku with twenty-first-century architecture makes for some memorable photos.

Upland Park

This green space *(Map F, Point 36)* is pretty much the highest point of Baku and is a beautiful and serene place to take a stroll. From the Funicular station, wander through the park with the Flame Towers on your right-hand side. There are many scenic spots to take photos. In particular, look out for the spectacular man-made waterfall feature.

Shehidlar Xiyabani (Martyr's Lane)

Located directly behind the waterfall, Martyr's Lane *(Map F, Point 37)* is a cemetery and memorial dedicated to those who died in two recent violent events, Black January and the Nagorno Karabakh War.

The cemetery has had a somewhat chequered past. It was established in 1918 as a Muslim cemetery, and initially contained the bodies of those killed in localised fighting of the Russian Civil War. However, when the Bolsheviks came to power in 1920, the cemetery was destroyed, the bodies removed and replaced by an amusement park. It was only after the collapse of the Soviet Union that the government reinstated the graveyard for the victims of recent conflicts.

Today, you can find the graves of 15,000 people here. White marble walls line the main central avenue, in front of which are black marble tombstones, each with a photo of the fallen. All have the same date of death - 20 January 1990 - the day of the Black January massacre. On this winter's weekend, the Soviet Red Army invaded Baku to quash a growing independence movement. Much cruelty accompanied the invasion, and historians estimate that the invaders killed three hundred. The atrocity only served to strength Azerbaijan's resolve, and the country achieved independence the following year.

Slightly further up the hill, in the shade of trees, are the graves of those killed in the Nagorno Karabakh War. This conflict lasted from 1988 to 1994 and saw ethnic Armenians of the Nagorno Karabakh region, backed by Armenia, fighting for independence from Azerbaijan. Over the years of persistent struggle, 30,000 people lost their lives. 1992 seems to have been a particularly bad year, as it repeatedly appears on the gravestones.

Shehidlar Monument

At the southeastern point end of the Martyrs Lane is the Shehidlar Monument *(Map F, Point 38)*, built in 1998 by the order of then-president Heydar Aliyev. This elegant open-sided tower stands over an eternal flame, issuing from a golden eight-pointed star. Another identical golden star on the apex of the monument's dome represents the spirits of those martyrs who sacrificed their lives for their country.

Dagustu Park

As you walk away from the monument, with the Caspian Sea on your right, you are now in Dagustu Park *(Map F, Point 39)*. The walkway along the ridge affords spectacular panoramic views of the city and sea. In the distance on the extreme left is the angular profile of the Baku Crystal Hall, built to host the Eurovision Song Contest, and the adjacent huge national flagpole. Looking further to the left you can take in the entire corniche, old city, business district and a big slice of the Absheron peninsula.

Once back down at the Bahram Gur Funicular station, you can begin the next perambulation, Corniche and Commerce.

PART 4 - Corniche and Commerce

Next to the statue of Bahram Gur is a subway leading under the busy Neftchilar Prospect. Once on the other side of the road, you are confronted with the distinctive shape of the Carpet Museum.

* * *

Map G | Carpet Museum and along Baku Boulevard

Carpet Museum

The Azerbaijan Carpet Museum *(Map G, Point 40)* was established in 1967 but has only just moved into its distinctive building, which takes the form of a gigantic carpet being rolled out, in 2014.

The museum is purportedly the only one in the world dedicated to the art of carpet weaving. It has the most extensive collection of Azerbaijani carpets anywhere, and safeguards for the nation more than 10,000 objects. Azerbaijani carpets are held dear to the heart of national culture, and UNESCO has recently declared that they are a "Masterpiece of Intangible Heritage". The museum plays a crucial role in their preservation and research and aims to further the knowledge of residents and visitors of this cultural treasure.

The museum takes its name from Latif Karimov, a scientist, artist and carpet weaver who showed how the carpet has the most profound connection to the history and culture of Azerbaijan. He made an immense contribution to the research and classification of carpets and led a revival in their making. The culmination of Karimov's work was the establishment of the museum in 1967. Twenty-six years later it was named after him.

Most of the carpets on display date from the seventeenth century onwards, and include flat-woven and pile carpets. A lot of information is presented as to how the carpets are made and how techniques and patterns differ between various regions. It is surprisingly fascinating, and while the notion of a carpet museum might bring up images of dusty, dull exhibitions, the opposite is the case. You can spend an informative couple of hours here.

In the basement of the museum is a small vault containing exquisite examples of Azerbaijan jewellery and metalwork, mostly from the last two hundred years but some from as far back as the bronze age.

The museum is open Tuesdays to Fridays from 10 am to 6 pm, with extended hours on Saturdays and Sundays from 10 am to 8 pm. The entrance fee is 7 Manat.

Little Venice

Directly in front of the Carpet Museum on the Corniche is Little Venice *(Map G, Point 41)*. Dating from the 1960s, this mini version of the glorious Italian city is replete with canals, elegant bridges, Venetian colonnades and, of course, gondolas. The town has two large islands and several small islets, each with a selection of restaurants, bars and cafes. It's a lovely venue for lunch and dinner, or merely to rest one's weary feet.

Bayraq

Walk 100 m north along the corniche. Here is the Bayraq *(Map G, Point 42)*, or national flagpole, not to be confused with another Bayraq at the southern end of the corniche, which once held the Guinness World Record as being the world's tallest flagpole. This bayraq faces the SOCAR building across the Neftchilar Prospect. Here, you can take Instagram-worthy photos of the national flag fluttering away with the Flame Towers in the background.

Azerbaijan's national flag is a blue-red-green tricolour with crescent moon and star in the middle and was adopted in 1918. However, the Bolshevik takeover in 1920 and subsequent integration into the Soviet Union meant that the flag didn't fly again until independence in 1991. The blue colour represents the Turkic origin and heritage of Azerbaijanis, the red symbolises modernisation and development, while the green expresses adherence to the Islamic religion. The crescent in the centre again links to Turkism, and the eight-pointed star refers to the eight guiding principles of the founder of the Azerbaijan Republic, Mammad Amin Rasulzade.

Baku Boulevard

From the flagpole, the wide Baku Boulevard and park *(Map G, Point 43)* runs parallel to Neftchilar Prospect and the shore of the Caspian Sea. This promenade traces its history back to the oil boom times in the late nineteenth century. At that time, Neftchilar Prospect was built to connect the oil fields in Bibi Heybat with the city. The oil barons built their mansions along one side, and the Caspian Sea was on the other. Over the years, the land on the seaward side was reclaimed inch by inch, with tons of fertile soil being imported to create the parkland seen today. The entire stretch now has National Park protected status and is a favourite place to stroll, jog, enjoy the fresh air and enjoy views of the sea and cityscape. Dotted along its length are pleasant cafes.

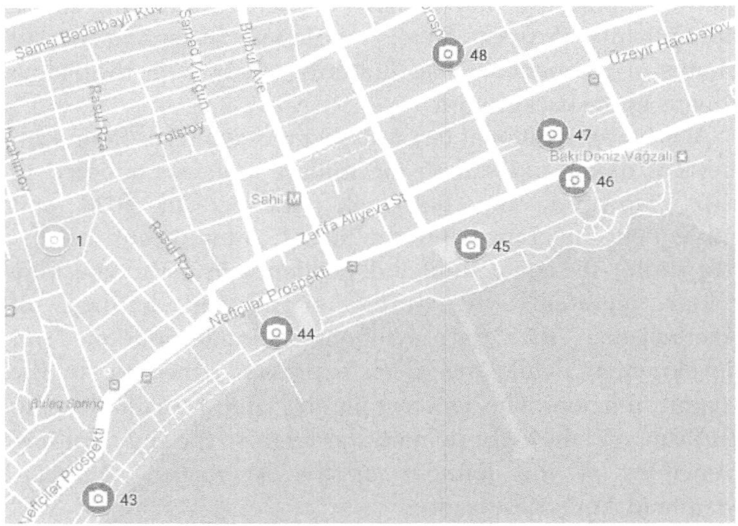

Map H | Baku Boulevard to Fountain Square

Halfway along the boulevard is the Parachute Tower *(Map H, Point 44)*, a 75 m high structure built in 1936 to resemble an oil derrick. Such towers were common at that time throughout the USSR, and as the name suggests were used for parachute jumping. Anyone could use it, not just the military, and you could opt to jump from ten, twenty, twenty-five or sixty-metre platforms, depending on your appetite for risk. Unfortunately, one of the jumpers died in an accident, and parachuting stopped soon after that. Nowadays, the tower is used to display the time, date, temperature and wind speed to those passing by underneath.

A five to ten-minute walk up the boulevard is the Park Bulvar shopping mall *(Map H, Point 45)*, offering high-end stores with many top brands.

Freedom Square and Government House

Just past the Park Bulvar mall is the Freedom Square *(Map H, Point 46)*, the biggest such public space in Baku. Built in the 1960s, the square was originally called Lenin Square and was home to a Lenin statue, removed after independence in 1991. The space now plays a vital role in the public life of Azerbaijan and hosts the annual independence day celebrations and military parades.

Fronting onto this square is the sprawling Stalinist bulk of Government House *(Map H, Point 47)*, built between 1936 and 1952 to house more than five thousand public servants. Today it is home to a variety of ministries, including those looking after tourism, agriculture, labour and procurement portfolios.

On either side of Government House are top-end hotels such as the Hilton and JW Marriott.

Retail therapy on Nizami Street

From Baku Boulevard, cross to the other side of Neftchilar Prospect using the pedestrian underpass found to the side of the Park Bulvar mall. Walk straight up Zadliq Prospect, past the Hilton Hotel, until you reach the junction with Nizami Street, at which point you should turn left.

Nizami Street *(Map H, Point 48)*, named after the famous Azerbaijani poet, is the most famous and glamorous shopping street of Baku, akin to London's Oxford Street or Paris' Champs Elysees. The real estate here is among some of the most expensive in the world. The main shopping area stretches from here all the way to Fountain Square, and as it is pedestrianised along its full length, it makes for a relaxing place to stroll and do some window shopping.

As well as the myriad retail opportunities, the other draw of Nizami Street is the architecture. Buildings here feature a variety of architecture including baroque, renaissance, neo-gothic and post-modern. There is something to please every taste.

Once you reach the ISR Plaza building, turn left, and after a few metres you will be in Fountain Square, where this walking tour concludes.

PART 5 - Day Trips from Baku

— Ateshgah Fire Temple —

The Ateshgah Fire Temple, further out on the Absheron peninsula, makes for a fascinating afternoon getaway from the city. It is an ancient site of Zoroastrian worship, and its name in Persian means 'Home of Fire'.

For centuries Zoroastrianism was the dominant religion of Azerbaijan, and evidence shows that it was extensively practised even as far back as the first millennium BC. The belief was also widespread in Iran before its eventual conversion to Islam. Once Azerbaijan became part of the Persian empire, various emperors such as Cyrus II and Darius I played an essential role in spreading Zoroastrianism across their empire. Even today, well-preserved temples can be seen in the Iranian cities of Yazd and Esfahan.

Zoroastrianism has the distinction of being the world's first monotheistic religion and takes its name from its founder, the Persian prophet Zoroaster. Adherents to the faith worshipped a god called Ahura Mazda, and fire was the most important symbol of the religion as it was considered to represent his holy spirit.

The Ateshgah fire temple complex is pentagonal. The five sides comprise a series of cells, chapels and a caravanserai, and these now house an exhibition that ponders the origin and purpose of the temple. In the middle of the central courtyard is the main fire temple altar, built directly over a natural gas vent.

The current form of this fire temple dates from the seventeenth century, although there is evidence that religious activity at this site stretched back much further in time. So why does this particular site hold so much importance to Zoroastrians? The answer is in the ground. This part of Azerbaijan has massive subterranean natural gas reserves, and in some place these bubble up to the surface and spontaneously combust into flame. For an ancient Zoroastrian, this would have seemed like a holy site, and followers would of course want to worship in such a place. Even today, just up the road at Yanar Dag, a hillside continues to burn due to this natural outpouring of gas.

After the introduction of Islam into the area, the ancient temples standing on this site were either destroyed or fell into ruin. However, activity at the site began to reoccur from the fifteenth century onwards, due to the strengthening of overland trade routes between the Caspian and the Subcontinent. Indian travellers and merchants soon made pilgrimages to the site, and at the turn of the eighteenth century began construction of religious buildings, some of which remain today. There is some dispute as to whether Zoroastrians or Hindus used the temple - fire is important to both religions - and displays inside the various cells and rooms of the temple complex present all sides of the argument. It is fascinating nonetheless to see a unique mix of

Sanskrit, Punjabi and Persian inscriptions throughout the temple.

In the mid-nineteenth-century, the gas supply became irregular due to geological movements, and the flame was no longer so constant. Worshippers took this as a sign of their god's displeasure, and they eventually abandoned the site in 1880. In the 1960s the gas ran out altogether, and the bright flames you see burning today are less romantically piped in by Baku's main gas supply.

Getting to Ateshgah Fire Temple

The temple *(Map I, Point 49)* is in the town of Surakhani, one of Baku's more farther-flung suburbs. The quickest way to get there is by hiring a taxi to take you directly there. You will need to negotiate with the driver to wait for you and then drop you back, as taxis are not easily found there, or will ask for high fares.

* * *

Map I | Ateshgah Fire Temple

However, a much more fun, and significantly cheaper option is to take public transport all the way there. It gives you a real insight into how ordinary Azerbaijanis go about their business each day and is a highlight of a visit to Baku. Here is a summary of how to do it:

- Catch a red line metro. In the centre of Baku, the most convenient stations are the Icherisheher (old town) next to the Philharmonic Park, and Sahil a couple of hundred metres east of Fountain Square. Make sure that the train is going in the direction of Hazi Aslanov.
- To get on the metro, you first need to by a 'Bakucard'

in the ticket hall. You can buy a card for extended use, which you can top up with cash, or one for limited use (1-4 rides). The cost of a ride is 0.20 AZN.

- Get off the train at Koroglu metro station. There are a few exits to this station, and you should make sure that you exit on the south side of the highway with traffic going away from the city (the Olympic Stadium is to the north)
- The Koroglu bus station is just the side of the highway with dozens of buses randomly parked all over the place. Look out for bus number 184 and hop on. The fare is 0.2 AZN. Don't worry about missing your stop. Just stay on until the bus route's terminus at Surakhani railway station.
- Cross the railway lines behind the station, looking out for the odd stray train as you do so!
- The Ateshgah Fire Temple is on your left at the end of the road.

Back to Baku

When returning to Baku, get another bus 184 from the same bus stop at the railway station. On the way back to the city the bus passes through a genuinely dystopian paradise of industrial-scale decay. Hundreds, if not thousands of rusting, poorly maintained 'nodding donkey' oil pumps line the road, interspersed with ageing electricity pylons and piles of discarded, oily machinery. If you are an environmentalist, it is best to look away. For movie buffs, this is where scenes of 'The World is Not Enough' was filmed, with Pierce Brosnan starring as secret agent James Bond. There are reports that local police are not keen on tourists taking photos were, so it is best to be discreet.

Once the bus stops at Koroglu metro station, get the red line back to the centre of town.

— Yanar Dag —

Yanar Dag *(Map J, Point 50)* is a dramatic natural gas flare which burns continuously on a hillside north of Baku between the villages of Digah and Mammedli. In Azerbaijani, the name Yanar Dag means burning mountainside. Flames shoot up between about 1 m and 2 m in the air and are particularly impressive at sunset or nighttime. The fire results from natural gas seeping out of the ground and then spontaneously combusting. There is a strong smell of gas in the air, and locals say that nearby streams can be ignited with a match. Maybe best not to smoke around here!

Such flames were once widespread throughout the Absheron peninsula, and Marco Polo even wrote about seeing them in the thirteenth century. These fires are the same phenomenon that once occurred at the site of the Ateshgah Fire Temple, and resulted in the spread of Zoroastrianism in the region. Today, due to the exploitation of oil and gas, reserves are much depleted, and Yanar Dag is now very much an oddity.

* * *

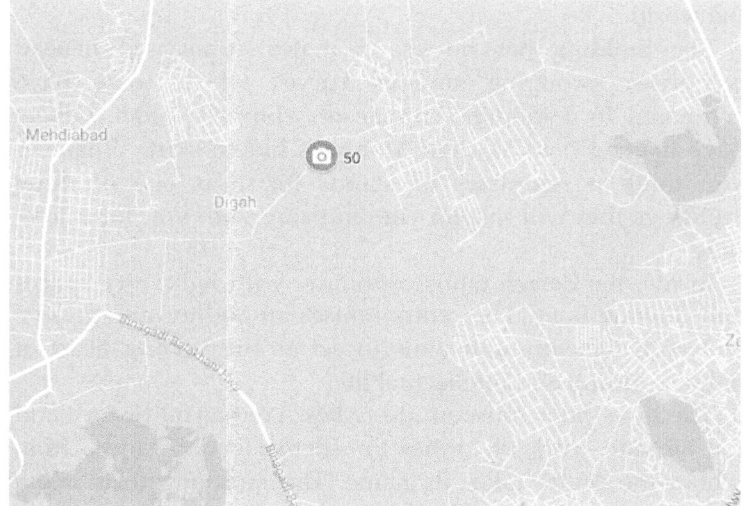

Map J: Yanar Dag

To get to Yanar Dag, you can catch a red line metro to Koroglu. Then take bus 217 from Koroglu metro station. Stay on the bus to its terminus. As both the Ateshgah Fire Temple and Yanar Dag are reached by different buses from this metro station, you could combine both destinations in one day trip.

— Heydar Aliyev Centre —

The Heydar Aliyev Centre *(Map K, Point 51)* is a mammoth cultural centre a bit out of the city centre towards the northeast. The building itself is a star attraction, and worth visiting even if you do not venture inside. The structure is designed by the lauded late architect, Zaha Hadid, and is regarded as one of her true masterpieces, even standing out from the many other fantastic buildings she created around the world.

The building has no sharp angles at all and instead comprises swooping sinuous curves which some have compared to a mountain range of whipped cream. Others have likened it to Marilyn Monroe's blown skirt. Whatever you think it resembles or stands for, it is one of those buildings that will inspire you and stay with you for a long time.

Inside, the design ethos continues, with light, airy spaces and flowing lines. The centre houses an auditorium, gallery, hall and museum, and aims to act as the beating heart of Baku's cultural and intellectual life.

The three-floor museum describes Azerbaijani history and the life and work of former President Heydar Aliyev, from whom the centre takes its name. The museum hosts many temporary exhibitions throughout the year.

* * *

Map K: Heydar Aliyev Centre

The Heyday Aliyev Centre is open from Tuesday to Sundays, from 11 am to 6 pm. A standard ticket, available online, costs 15 Manat. To get there from the centre of Baku, there are frequent services on a variety of bus lines, including buses 1 and 2. Visit www.bakubus.az for the latest routes and timetables; the site is available in English.

— Gobustan National Park —

Located 60 km southwest of Baku, this national park is famed for two things you are unlikely to find elsewhere on your travels: petroglyphs and mud volcanoes. The park is an easy day trip from the city, and you can use one of the many travel agencies offering tours there, or hire a taxi.

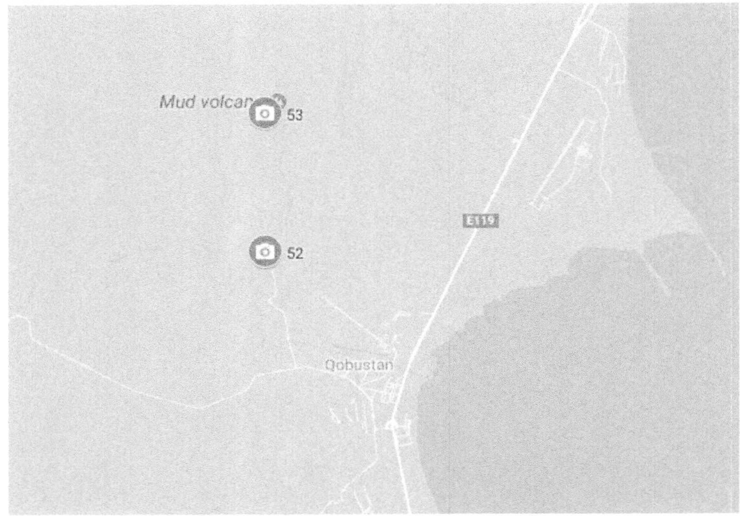

Map L | Gobustan National Park

Petroglyphs (Map L, Point 52)

Petroglyphs are drawings, etched into rock outcrops, by our prehistoric ancestors. In Gobustan, the land is sliced through with deep ravines, or gobu in Azerbaijani, and some liken it to a "sea of rocks". The discovery of the petroglyphs in the 1930s here was a matter of pure chance. The area was being exploited for stone quarrying, when one day a worker noticed some strange paintings on a rock face. Archaeologists over the years have uncovered another six thousand such pictures, the earliest of which date back all the way to the tenth century BC.

The rock images depict humans, bulls, lions, deer, horses and many more animals, some of them life-size. Others give a valuable insight into civilisation during that time, showing labour practices, battle scenes, dancing and more.

The first place to visit upon reaching the park is the museum. The dozen or so rooms display photographs of some of the most important petroglyphs and give in-depth interpretations of the pictures. The museum also tells the story of the discovery of the petroglyphs and of the subsequent research and analysis.

A five-minute drive from the museum you enter the petroglyph reserve itself. Here you can walk through the gorges and view the petroglyphs in situ. Some are very prominent and easy to spot, whereas others might take a bit more patience to find. It is a stimulating exercise to try to decipher the meaning of each. English speaking guides are available to help you get the most out of your visit.

Mud volcanoes (Map L, Point 53)

There are around one thousand mud volcanoes in the world, and four hundred of these are in Azerbaijan. Many of these are located in the Gobustan region, just a short drive away from the petroglyph park. However, don't worry. Unlike regular volcanoes, these are not thousands of metres high spouting hot lava and ash clouds. Instead, they are like oversized molehills, about a metre or two high, and at the top of each mud slowly bubbles and plops in a pool much like a giant mud bath.

Mud volcanoes are an unmistakable sign of subterranean oil and gas deposits, which explains why there are so many in Azerbaijan. The mud originated from deep underground, where water is heated and mixed with mineral deposits. This slurry is then driven through cracks and fissures by subterranean pressure imbalances until it eventually emerges to form the volcano. On occasion, perhaps every twenty years or so, things liven up a bit with spontaneous combustion of methane gas many hundreds of metres high. Such eruptions could be the reason Zoroastrianism became such a widespread religion in these parts.

The volcanic mud appears to have medical benefits and can be used to treat central and peripheral nervous disorders and diseases of the skin and digestive tract. It is also thought to be great for younger looking skin!

When driving around this area keep a look out for wet, black patches in the desert. This is where oil is seeping unbidden out of the ground. It's not pollution but rather a natural process.

PART 6 - Preparing for your visit

— Essential info —

When to visit

Azerbaijan has a continental influenced climate. However, the presence of the Caspian Sea and the nearby Caucasus mountains makes the country climatically diverse, and nine out of the eleven recognised climate types are present in the country.

However, it is possible to make some generalisations for a visit to Baku. Days during spring and autumn are pleasantly fresh and crisp, with nights becoming quite chilly. During the winter, temperatures vary between around 5C to 10C, with occasional icy conditions at night. Summer is the best time to visit with warm, sunny conditions and temperatures hovering around 32C, although it may feel hotter due to high humidity.

Rainfall is relatively low, averaging five rainy days each month. However, in the summer months from May to September, rain is much more scarce.

* * *

Visas

Azerbaijan has a relatively relaxed visa regime. Almost 100 nationalities can apply for an e-visa online from the official Republic of Azerbaijan Visa Portal, evisa.gov.az. The cost is USD 20, and it takes three working days to process. Citizens of most western European countries, Gulf states, Australia, New Zealand, Japan, Korea and Singapore, can use this service. For all other nationalities, it is necessary to apply for a visa in advance at an Azerbaijani embassy.

Currency

The currency is the Azerbaijani Manat (AZN). Each Manat splits into 100 Gepik. At the time of writing, February 2018, one US Dollar bought 1.69 Manat, one British Pound bought 2.36 Manat, and one Euro got 2.08 Manat. You can easily exchange these main currencies in the city, and exchanges and banks are commonplace. ATMs also accept Visa, Visa Electron, Mastercard and Maestro cards.

Time Zone

Baku is in the Azerbaijaini Time (AZT) zone, which is GMT+4. The country does not currently observe daylight savings time.

* * *

Electricity

Azerbaijan's electricity is of the 220V/50Hz variety. The wall sockets take plugs with two round pins. Take a range of adaptors with you to make sure you can connect.

— Getting There and Away —

By Air

Baku has one airport serving all international and domestic airlines. Heydar Aliyev International Airport (GYD) is about a 20 km drive northeast of the city centre, further out on the Absheron peninsula. It is the busiest airport in Azerbaijan and the whole of the Caucasus region, with a wide range of routes spanning the Middle East, Europe, Russia and America.

Here are the airlines currently connecting **international destinations** with Baku:

- Aeroflot has daily flights to Moscow Sheremetyevo, with onward connections on its services and those of the SkyTeam Alliance. www.aeroflot.com
- Air Arabia links Baku with Sharjah daily. www.airarabia.com
- Air Astana flies to Almaty and Astana. www.airastana.com
- Azerbaijan Airlines offers the widest selection of destinations from Baku, including New York JFK, Beijing, Sharjah, Dubai, Kuwait, Baghdad, Tehran,

Istanbul, Ankara, Antalya, Tbilisi, Tel Aviv, London Heathrow, Paris, Milan, Lviv and Kiev. Russian destinations include Moscow Domedodovo, Moscow Vnukovo, St. Petersburg and Kazan. www.azal.az

- China Southern flies to Urumqi twice a week. www.csair.com
- Etihad flies to Abu Dhabi. www.etihad.com
- FlyDubai offers flights ten times a week to its Dubai hub, with onward connections around the Middle East, Africa, the Subcontinent, the Caucasus and Europe. www.flydubai.com. Alternatively, passengers can connect to Emirates' global network.
- Lufthansa has flights to both Ashgabat and Frankfurt. www.lufthansa.com
- Iran Air www.iranair.com and Mahan Air www.mahan.aero fly to Tehran, Iran.
- Iraqi Airways connects Baku to Baghdad and Najaf. www.iraqiairways.com.iq
- Israir flies to Tel Aviv twice a week. www.israir.co.il
- Jazeera Airways goes to Kuwait twice a week. www.jazeeraairways.com
- Pegas Fly has a daily flight to Moscow Zhukovsky airport www.pegasfly.ru
- Qatar Airways has double daily flights to its hub at Doha, from where you can connect to its global network. One of these daily flights also stops off at Tbilisi. www.qatarairways.com
- S7 flies to Novosibirsk and Moscow Domodedovo. www.s7.ru
- Turkish Airlines has a flight to Istanbul four times every day. From its Istanbul hub, you can fly just about anywhere in the world. www.turkishairlines.com
- Ukraine International Airlines flies to Kiev.

www.flyuia.com

- Ural Airlines flies to Yekaterinburg twice a week. www.uralairlines.com
- UT Air goes to Surgut and Moscow Vnukovo. www.utair.ru
- Uzbekistan Airlines links Tashkent to Baku. www.uzairways.com
- Wataniya links Baku with Kuwait three times a week. www.wataniyaairways.com
- Wizz Air flies to Budapest once a week. www.wizzair.com

As Azerbaijan is quite a small country, there are not too many services to other cities domestically. However, Azerbaijan Airlines flights connect the **domestic** destination of Ganja with Baku three times a week.

By Rail

There is a relatively extensive railway network in Azerbaijan, comprising almost 3000 km of track and 176 stations.

Baku is connected to several international destinations, including Moscow, Tbilisi, Kharkov and Rostov, as well as many other Russian cities.

Domestically, tracks cross pretty much the whole country, including the entire Caspian Sea coast, the southern border with Iran, and central and northwestern regions. The fare is unlikely to exceed more than USD 5 anywhere in the country.

Tickets can be purchased online on the Azerbaijan Railways website, https://ticket.ady.az/en. The site also has full timetable and route information, displayed in English.

By Road

The most straightforward route is from Tbilisi in Georgia. An overnight bus service takes about eight hours. Buses leave from the Avtovagsal bus station in the northwest of the city.

To the north, it is also possible to go by road to Russia, although current security concerns in Dagestan makes this option inadvisable. To the south, the Astara border crossing with Iran can be reached by taxi or bus in about five hours. To the west, the border with Armenia is closed.

By Boat

Baku can be reached by ferry from Turkmenbashi in Turkmenistan. The journey takes about seventeen hours, with boats leaving every day or every other day. There is also a ferry service from Aktau in Kazakhstan, a trip taking thirty hours and with departures every three to five days.

The term 'ferry' should actually translate as old, rusting cargo ship. The schedules are informal at best and are dictated by loading and by the mechanical readiness of the vessel itself. Therefore, this option is best for adventurous souls with plenty of time on their hands.

— Getting Around —

From the airport

The most convenient and cheapest way of getting to the city centre is by the Aero Express service, which operates modern 48-seater coaches. These leave every 30 minutes throughout the day, except between 9 pm and 5 am when it reverts to an hourly frequency. The journey to the 28 May metro station and central railway station takes thirty minutes and costs 1.5 AZN. Cash is not accepted on board these buses, and you need to buy a BakuCard from a kiosk in the terminal, so ensure you have some local currency available.

For taxis, follow signs for 'Official Taxis' and book with one of the marshalls. The official taxis are white London taxis, and the journey should cost 25 AZN. It is best to ignore the many men offering taxis as soon as you walk out of the terminal.

The metro does not currently serve the airport. However, from the city centre to the airport you could get a red line metro to Koroglu, where you can pick up one of the many taxis to take you to the airport for about 10 AZN.

Around the city

As explained in the detailed walking tours in this guide, the majority of sights are accessible on foot. However, for when feet get tired, or if the weather is not cooperating, the good news is that there are extensive public transport networks. These are supported by well-designed websites, available in English, with maps and routes all easily accessible to make journey planning a breeze.

The metro and bus networks operate on a cashless basis, and to use them you first need to get a BakuCard. Vending machines are at the airport, in all metro stations and at some bus stops. You can buy an extended use card for 2 Manat which you can then top up as much as you like. Alternatively, you can purchase limited use cards for between one to four journeys. All one-way rides on buses and metros, regardless of length, cost 0.20 Manat, making it one of the cheapest public transport networks in the world.

Baku's metro system operates from 6 am to midnight with trains running at a frequency of every two to three minutes. There are two lines, with the red line linking Icherisheher with Hazi Aslanaov, and the Green line connecting Khatai to Darnagul. The central interchange is 28 May station. Trains and stations are safe and clean. Listen for the pieces of music played before arrival at each station...each has been specially chosen for its relevance to that stop. For more information on the metro, visit www.metro.gov.az/en.

Baku's bus network spreads its tentacles across the entire city, out into the suburbs and across the Absheron peninsula. They can take you just about anywhere you want to go. Note that the buses no longer accept money and passengers should use the Bakucard. For full information on buses, visit www.bakubus.az/en.

Finally, you will see taxis cruising everywhere around Baku, and you can easily hail one from the street. The London taxi cabs have meters, with each kilometre costing 0.70 Manat. To hire other taxis you will need to negotiate. Perhaps the most convenient option is Uber, which now operates in the city.

— Where to stay —

Due to its oil and gas industry, and thriving economy, Baku is jammed with top-end accommodation options. However, by booking early you can still get good deals, and there are many other options at all levels. Here are just a few highlights in the top end and mid-range categories, however www.booking.com lists all the possible options at the competitive rates. Furthermore, Tripadvisor.com compares prices with the three or four top hotel consolidators, making sure you get the most reasonable rate. There is also a wide selection of apartments and rooms to rent in Baku on www.airbnb.com.

Top end

Hyatt Regency Baku is in a quiet part of Baku about a 25-minute walk from Fountain Square. Huge, comfortable rooms and excellent facilities include two 25 m swimming pools - one inside and one outside.

Fairmont Baku can be seen from all over Baku, as it's in one of the iconic Flame Towers. Facilities include six dining options, a spa, and rooftop and indoor swimming pools. You also get direct access to the Flame Towers complex, with many restaurants, bars, shops and an IMAX cinema.

Four Seasons Baku has quite possibly one of the best locations in the city, in a lavish building right on the Baku Boulevard, a stone's throw away from the Maiden Tower and Old Town. It has become the place to see and be seen in Baku and is frequented by wealthy and high profile guests.

JW Marriott Absheron is well situated next to Freedom Square and Government House, near to Baku Boulevard. There's a variety of restaurants and bars, an indoor swimming pool and on-site fitness centre.

Hilton Baku is directly across Freedom Square from the JW Marriott, handy for the main Nizami shopping street.

* * *

Mid-range

Park Inn by Radisson is just across Neftchilar Prospect from the Park Bulvar Mall. This good value option has all the facilities of its more expensive counterparts, including modern rooms, free Wi-Fi, fitness centre and good in-house dining options.

Holiday Inn Baku is in a bustling commercial and business area just east of Freedom Square. Guests rate the hotel for its modern, spacious rooms.

Qafqaz Baku City Hotel is an ultra-modern, highly-rated four-star option in a quiet area a short taxi ride away from the centre. In addition to the usual facilities, it has a sun terrace and spa with hot spring bath.

Bristol Hotel Baku is just a few steps from the Old Town in a cosy old building. Some of the double rooms come with a balcony. The hotel is one of the top-rated value for money options in Baku.

The Old Street Boutique Hotel is located right next to the Old Town city and is rated number one amongst Baku B&B and Inns on TripAdvisor. It's only got eleven rooms, so you need to book well in advance.

Index

A

B

C

* * *

L

M

N

O

* * *

Y

Copyright

FewDaysAway

PO Box 215878
Dubai
United Arab Emirates

www.fewdaysaway.com

This edition published 2018.

Printed in Great Britain
by Amazon